Pearl Harbor For Kids

DISCOVER THIS CHILDREN'S BOOK ABOUT PEARL HARBOR WITH FACTS

No part of this book may be reproduced or used in any way or form or by any means whether electronic or mechanical, this means that you cannot record or photocopy any material ideas or tips that are provided in this book.

Copyright 2019

Pearl Harbor was how the US got into the second world war. Here are the interesting facts about pearl harbor for you to learn.

The Pearl Harbor attack was actually launched in 2 waves around 42 minutes apart and lasted over 106 minutes.

While they did travel over 3,250 miles to execute the attack, they were actually only less then 245 miles north of Oahu before they attacked.

They chose to attack on a Sunday since they believed Americans would be less alert during the weekend.

The Japanese only chose to attack Pearl Harbor ships and the ones at Hickman Airfield, which left repair facilities and fuel oil storage areas not harmed.

All of the US battleships were sunk during the attack, but all but two of them were able to return to active duty eventually

The Japanese didn't just have airplanes, but subs as well to target the battleships. The US managed to capture four and sunk the fifth one

Survivors of the attack actually are given a choice to join their comrades there as the final resting place, choosing to have their ashes deposited below one of the turrets of the Arizona

There are just a few of the survivors currently still living today of this horrific event that took place decades ago.

The USS Arizona, the only one that wasn't brought back, still leaks fuel today, and it spills over 8.5 quarts of it into the harbor each day

There are actually remains of a baby girl within the sunken battleship, which was left on the USS Utah to be scattered but the scattering wasn"t done

Pearl Harbor was a pretty significant attack, and here you learned facts about this.

Ingram Content Group UK Ltd.
Milton Keynes UK
UKHW050640190523
422014UK00005B/20